How We Named Our Cats

V. R. AGNELLI

ISBN-10: 0615903584
ISBN-13: 978-0615903583

DEAR READER,

This book is dedicated to my Wife and the love she has brought to my life and to all of the little and not so little creatures that God has put on our world to live with us. To name a few, Mei Li, Nina, Zorba, Chloie, Blackie, Marshall, Buddietta, Smudgy, Smokey , Sunny and Buffy.

CONTENTS

ACKNOWLEDGMENTS

Special thanks to teachers Nancy Oliver and Ed Petty of Lake Braddock Secondary and Dr. Charles Scarborough of the Northern Virginia Community College. My endeavor into changing careers was aided by your efforts and teaching from many years ago. Without a doubt, Oliver and Petty were the great motivators and Scarborough is the great emancipator of our English language.

"You can't save all of them but if you can help

some of them then save as many as you can."

---- *V. R. Agnelli*

1

THE FIRST TEST:
FROM SUBURBAN TO RURAL

It was late February 2002, when we knew we were approved for the purchase of our "fixer upper" in the country. Spring was still a long way from showing what she could offer in a bounty of wild flowers and colorful pollen pods on the trees. We planned a great deal of restoration work to be finished before we could even move into this house. The horse paddocks were a wreck and the fencing needed complete replacement. The barn had three stalls filled with manure and weeds were everywhere.

There was a tractor on order from the factory and a good number of implements to help with all the jobs around the place. Especially with those jobs that required heavy-duty equipment. It would not arrive until April so those types of chores would have to wait a while for completion.

Our house was another story in that it needed a completely new heating and air-conditioning system, water heater, plumbing fixtures and a new well pump. One might say, we should have just razed the house and started over. You can bet if we had enough money to start from scratch we would have.

One of the things we never considered when moving to a rural area was the stray animal population. The cats and dogs, which run wild in the country, are a terrible thing to contemplate and you can react in either one of two ways when confronted with them. You can ignore them and hope they go away or you can befriend them and try to make a safe haven for them.

Some folks try to bring them into their homes and others try to keep them going in their outbuildings. If you feed them and try to get them basic veterinary care, you are just being a compassionate human being and not a sucker. You acquire "sucker" status when you feed so many animals that they all need a name!

We were going out on the weekends to work on the place so we could move in by our targeted date in April. On several occasions, we had seen a black cat around the house and in the barn and we expected to see it again in our travels though we had not seen it every time we went out to work on the house.

When we first closed the deal and settled on the house, we were aware the previous owners were looking for one of their cats who had run off because the movers scared her. We never knew if they found her or not so, the work began of remodeling the house immediately and without another thought since we had no description of the lost cat.

On our second trip to the house, we brought our Dalmatian "Zorba". Zorba was getting on in age, about 12 years old if I recall. He was getting a little blind but his nose and ears worked just fine. He could not see a cat

2

any more but he knew the smell of one.

We had some fence lumber delivered right away and it was sitting under one of those blue tarps that you buy at the big box stores or a hardware store. As we exited our SUV, Zorba walked over to that lumber pile and started sniffing around the edges. We walked over to see what had peaked Zorba's interest. It was a small kitty with an obvious distended belly from starvation. It had a thin coat of multi-colored hair and it hissed at Zorba as he got near. The kitty could muster the strength to get up over three or four inches of boards but that was all.

I was concerned it might be sick and recommended to have it "put down". My wife who has been an animal lover from childhood, just about verbally sent me back into the previous week of the calendar! My wife walked around the back of the house with our cooler and I with my tools for the day's work. The little kitty followed her and rubbed against my wife's legs. The kitty rubbed against the cooler because it made a noise with the ice sloshing around in it but it must have had a residual smell of food, which attracted it to it.

I went down to the local general store and picked up some generic cat food in cans and dry form and returned to see my wife sitting with the little kitty in one of the plastic lawn chairs we brought along for moments of rest and lunch breaks. With a paper plate of some food, the little kitten gorged and gorged her way to a full stomach. It was obvious a life had been saved and the void in my wife's conscious left by the passing of her fifteen-year-old cat Nina, just a year before, was now being filled with her plans to help this little soul.

We had been worried about not living there during the restoration period and what would come of the little dear without us having the house open? The stables were in a wreck but they did offer secure shelter from the elements and we set up an area in the tack room where we fed her and gave her a cat bed to sleep in.

In the following weeks as March turned to April and the light of day was getting longer, we made mid-week trips to the house just to feed the little kitten. We were never sure it was going to stick around so we never really thought of giving it a name.

We started to see the black cat more often and many times, we would see the black cat and the kitty together. The kitty by now was showing signs of actually being an adult cat that was just so emaciated it looked about the size of a kitty. We could not tell if the black cat was showing the other cat how to hunt, but we noticed it was not the most agile of cats and had poor skeletal confirmation. All of that was made up by her ability to show thanks and affection for taking care of her (something she never stopped showing for the rest of her life).

Moving day came in April. After we moved all of our worldly possessions into the house, we would spend our first night in our halfway remodeled home. The downstairs would have to be a "work in progress" as time went on, but a room downstairs which was not in bad condition, would be turned over to our new cat friend, from outside.

The kitty was still around, but the black cat never seemed to be around when you were looking for it. By this time, it had occurred to us that this little female cat had been somebody's pet that got loose. We speculated that she might be the cat of the former owner and she simply hung around waiting for them to return, but there was no way for us to confirm that. She was used to our being around and we decided it was time to make her ours.

She was still suffering from fleas and she would not let just anybody get close to her. Whenever we would bring food out to the barn, we would see her hiding behind some old pieces of plywood, only to emerge when we laid out the food. Then she would come out and rub up against my wife's legs. It was clear there was a friendship brewing there but I was still cautious.

2
A CAT IS SAVED AND GETS A NAME

On the day we decided to take our newfound friend in as an indoor pet, we scheduled a trip to the local veterinarian for a checkup and shots. This is always one of those hurdles that can break your heart. Therefore, we held out hope and said our prayers she would come through without a hitch.

Once that was over, we brought her home and placed her into this downstairs room, which had a combination of furniture and boxes in it. We added a couple of empty boxes with towels and of course, a litter box, water and food.

She kept her affinity for hiding in dark places and when we came into the room, she would hide. This lasted for almost two weeks and we were getting concerned that she would not adapt to inside life. Then one day she stayed outside of her hole in the boxes to watch me place her food down in a bowl. She did not move to eat it until I had turned away and was walking out of the room. This progressed in a few days to her trusting me not to try anything tricky, as she would start to eat as soon as I put the food down.

It was after a week of this that one day, before I moved away from her and the food bowl; she swung her tail around and gently rubbed it across my forearm. She had made the first contact and in a day or so, I would pet her tail, as she would eat.

As time would go on and we let her out of the room into the rest of the house to interact with Zorba, she would still run and hide in that room. She felt safe there and almost preferred to be cloistered away from all people and things. This gave me my first thought on how to name this little creature. This behavioral characteristic looked to be rich with naming possibilities.

I liked the idea of giving her a name based on a psychological characteristic rather than a person's name. Her hair coloring was multicolored but not as defined as a Calico so there was trouble using a physical prompt for a name. I could not use "Cloistered" for a name yet that was her main characteristic, which stood out. Also, one has to remember, cats prefer names that end in an "ie" or "y" sound.

As it turned out, there are not too many words, which described this characteristic and could be changed into those endings. I decided it was time to make it "an inside joke". It was a tale that would have to be told every time somebody would ask about her name. Therefore, it became "Chloie". We would know her as "Chloie the Cloistered Kitty" or "Chloie".

She was always a good sport about it and she bonded with our dog better than anything I have ever witnessed of the kind between a cat and a dog.

3

One Story Ends And Another One Begins

A handful of years passed from the time we newlyweds moved into our home. We had only just begun to see the fruits of our hard work on our home when Zorba, who at almost fifteen years of age, became quite ill one afternoon. He came to me while I was working on a door latch and started to shake. He lost control of his bodily functions and then fell to the floor in violent convulsions. Chloie paced nervously around behind me, in a fashion of concern and not fear. I could tell because if my "Cloistered Kitty" were ever afraid of anything, she would run for her hideout. She was concerned for her big dog friend and knew he was not well.

After a terrible trip to the veterinarian some 25 miles away, we had the answer to the question of when it was going to be Zorba's time. We brought his body back home and instinctively my wife knew where to inter him. It was in the middle of group of old white dogwood trees, whose shade he used to always lay down in during the summer months, as he would watch us work on the fences or the driveway or just cutting the lawn. We also felt his spirit would always be watching out for us at the entrance, as he always did at the front door.

Zorba was a special dog, in that he had been with my wife for ten years before we met and then married. His tale is better left for another time and another book but I cannot leave this moment without paying respect to his intelligence and loyalty. I respected his judgment in what can only be identified as "Socratic" when judging people. He will always be on our minds as time marches on.

Chloie was alone now and she knew Zorba was missing. Since they both shared the same water bowl, we decided not to change out the big dog-sized bowl for a while. It was during this period that Chloie would get even closer to us and in a way that only pictures and stories could reveal. However, the dynamics of time were still changing as the vacuum left that early spring by Zorba's loss would be filled a year later.

One April morning, the next year, we noticed a striped tail through the partial view behind a wood box on our back deck. The cat who lived in the barn was a black shorthaired female whom we had named "Blackie" after my wife's parent's cat. I rather rushed through that here because it was not a hard name to give. We did not use much imagination and Blackie got her name after we brought Chloie inside. We never really considered her our cat, since she lived outside, but we did care for her and she spent just as much time at the vet's office as any other cat I know. Her domain was the barn and the grounds; we always allowed her to maintain her reign without restrictions. This new "tail" was something else altogether. It belonged to a half grown kitten!

She was by herself and did not look to be afraid of much. She looked to be in full control of her environment, which meant she was so new to our back deck that she had not met up with Blackie as of yet. Her coat was surprisingly shiny and was a classic Tabby scheme. The base color was a dark fawn with her stripes and spine in black. She had a great white bib, which stopped halfway down her front and then returned on the top of her paws as if it was paint that had flowed behind the other colors on her legs and run back out again over her little paws.

She was just as cute as could be with a round little "pumpkin" face and almond shaped eyes. Her tail was one of the longest tails I'd ever seen on a cat. She was watching over the back yard, as a hunter would sit in a tree blind in anticipation of catching sight of some prey.

The creature was amusing to us and we figured Blackie would have her cast off in no time but, as I mentioned, my wife loves animals. It was not but a minute passing by that she had a little paper plate with some cat food on it, in hand and slowly walking it through our back door, to be laid down in a non-threatening manner for the little cat to see.

Chloie and I were not too sure of this. I was just thinking of "how are we going to afford more vet bills?" and Chloie was just getting used to having all of the attention from us. She went to the glass door and made sure the new arrival understood not to even think about coming inside her house via her delivery of a siren like scream!

Well, the little cat would occasionally "get into it" with Blackie. One time they even became locked together and tumbled across the lawn some five times before my loud clapping and yelling broke up the fight.

We had been feeding Blackie in the barn and my wife had been feeding the new cat on the deck, so at least during feeding times, they would be separated and for the most part, they stayed clear of each other.

That spring turned into summer quickly and the new cat was getting to be a fixture on my legs. In fact, I trained her to come to me like a dog when I would whistle! She still does it to this day.

She was a tree climber in a way I have never seen before. She would shoot straight up a sixty foot oak tree in our front paddock that had no limbs below ten feet and then she would run right back down the tree! Most cats will try to climb down a tree when they want to come down but not this little scrambler. No, she would run down the tree and transition to the ground just as smoothly as if she was running on straight ground. Here again, I thought this would be the behavior we would try to capture with a name. "Dynamics" would once again take control of events and her name was about to come from a completely different place.

4

THE "WEB" OF A NAME

Lodging the cats was becoming an issue, as were feeding places. We had been feeding the new cat on the deck but it was becoming so attached to us that it wanted to be with us in whatever little detail of work or pleasure we had planned. As we were feeding Blackie in the tack room portion of the barn, we had to take up the end horse stall and feed the new cat on a stack of lumber and hay we were temporarily keeping there.

It was not long before Blackie was fine with that arrangement, as long as she was fed first. The little cat wasn't afraid of the horses but our Quarter horse Beary, was a little less fond of this leg-rubbing creature. Our Quarter-Thoroughbred cross horse Marshall, was not intimidated by cats. Blackie's time with us, up to this point, had shown she liked running around on the top sections of the barn and over the stalls where she wisely would avoid getting a kick from a horse. We would have to work on this with the new cat before it became a problem.

We decided to buy a cat basket and a cat tunnel for her

to use and make a home out of, so that she might get used to being around the horses and watching Blackie for tips on how to move around the barn.

After a short period, it was looking to be a good solution to our worries about the new cat's safety. She was exploring all around the barn and finding new paths around the items we had stored there.

One afternoon we were entertaining a friend and had gone outside to show her our new cat and the tricks she could do. The little cat came slowly out of the barn upon my whistling for her. She was not excited to see me as usual, but instead, almost looked in a daze. As she came closer, I could see a bit of her hair sticking up, mid-way down her back. As she got close to me, she sat down on my foot and made a weak sounding meow. I ran my hand down the back of her head and to that spot in question. It was a lump in a spot where there wasn't one that morning.

I was quite concerned but it was a Sunday and the vet's office was closed. The nearest emergency vet was that same office we had to take Zorba and the memories were just too much to bear but if we had to, we would take her in regardless.

With the help of our friend, we decided she should spend some time inside for the night where we could keep a closer eye on her. It was a decision that saved her life and brought us to her name.

Later that evening my wife went down to look after the new cat. It was not a few seconds after I heard her close the downstairs bathroom door that I heard her voice shouting up the stair case, "Honey, you better get down here!". That part of my chivalry training from my father made me stop everything I was doing and rush to the sound of my wife's voice. I ran down the steps at top speed and flung open the door to the downstairs bathroom to see a very sick kitty.

Our house was built in 1973 and it was a well-apportioned and equipped house for its day. One of the things I liked about it being in the country is that it had a septic system, which perks for three full bathrooms. This downstairs bathroom was all original with fixtures and wallpaper. The color of the sink, toilet and tub were the very popular Marigold motif complete with matching checked floor tile. One can say that these choices may not work so well in our modern world of "gray", but I can testify as to their hardiness when it comes to cleaning up messes. Our new cat was about to leave us one to clean up.

As it turned out that evening, the lump on her back became huge. It was no longer just under her hair, but in a matter of just a few hours, it had grown to the size of a golf ball and her hair was so stretched, her skin was visible. She was obviously ill and just sitting on some towels we set up for her to use as a bed. She was just making little crying sounds and an occasional whimper. We knew it was time to take her to the emergency vet and my wife sent me out to find the carrier.

I could have only been gone a minute and when I had my hands on the carrier, she opened the door and called back to me to bring some more towels and some cleaning chemicals. Items in hand and only another minute added to the tab, I walked back in the door only to see the cat sitting back up and licking its back. The lump was all but gone, my wife was using the towels the cat had been sitting on to clean up blood, and tissue from what had been the cat's lump. It had burst right in front of my wife but thankfully not on her.

The pressure relief was obvious, as the cat looked

better. We decided to keep her in the bathroom overnight for observation. The Marigold tile cleaned up wonderfully, grout and all. We would look in on her one more time before going to bed.

The wife and I sat up for hours trying to figure out just what caused this lump on her back. We did not have high-speed internet out that way yet and even then, there was not a lot of content on the web about every subject as we have today. We just had to play this one "by ear".

It was time to go to bed and that meant one more check on the little one. It was a good thing we did. The lump had started to grow back right next to where it originally came up. We knew what was going to be the result of that and infection became a concern. Therefore, with great disappointment, we loaded the new cat up and headed out the door in the middle of the night for that 25-mile drive we knew so well.

This particular veterinarian office was a large multi-doctor business with two levels, operating rooms, separate waiting areas for cat etc. We don't use them anymore because the growth of our area brought new veterinarians further out and they have facilities, which fit our needs. However, if we ever needed it we knew were to go in the middle of the night.

There we were with a doctor, at 2:30 AM, getting the diagnosis. She had been bitten on the back by a spider, not once but twice! The bites were leaving deep wounds of infection, which were most like those left by the Brown Recluse Spider. We lived in the country so that was no shock to us since Black Widows grow like weeds out there.

The surgery was to remove a patch of skin some 4 inches long and one inch wide down the middle of her back. There were drainage tubes poking out of each end of the suture that looked painful and very unnatural. We were assured that she was going to come through and the vet told us she would not have made it had she been left outside to fend for herself.

Then the vet asked us if she was an inside cat. Immediately upon answering her question with the details, the vet said and I can quote, "It's time to make her one". With that kind of advice, I can see how the balance between common sense on judging how many in the home is too many with regard to cats. It is a tough nut to crack when you have so many running around who just want a good meal and place to sleep out of the elements.

We could not bring her home just yet. The infection needed to be brought under control and it would take a few days. The paper work asked for her name and we had been so stressed out by the events that any thought of a name escaped us. For the moment, she was listed under "stray". Driving back home the arachnophobia, which I share with my wife, still haunted me. Those spiders were in my barn, I was going to go through that place with every chemical known to mankind and kill every one of them, and that is how the name for this new cat came to me, from that thought of the spiders.

E. B. White's 1952 storybook "Charlotte's Web" was a perfect reminder of a life saved. Though these spiders were of a different nature from his story, giving the cat the name of the good Spider from the barn in White's book might help to keep the bad spirits away.

Charlotte, is now the most talkative, possessive and sometimes impish little creature you have ever seen in a cat. She would get into more trouble along the way even though she lives exclusively inside. She now has two inches of her tail missing thanks to a "childproof" blind cord. However, she is our Charlotte whose name will always bring to mind, the tales of her spry days as an outside cat.

5
CHLOIE GETS A NICKNAME

Before getting to the naming of the other litters, I must add the story of giving Chloie a "nick- name". I do not know of many animals that can identify themselves with two names, but as we found with Chloie, she was an exceptional animal. She loved attention, which gave us the room to use another name for her. She no doubt took it as a form of action like Pavlov's dog, but we made great use of it.

After we brought Charlotte inside and began to groom her to be a companion to Chloie, there was a period of concern. This young, spry and impish little cat was too much for Chloie to bear. Chloie would run and hide and we might not see her but for feeding time. We tried to get them together but it just wasn't working. Chloie would not defend herself against the playful advances of Charlotte.

After some time, we noticed Chloie was getting sick with her food and more to the point; it precipitated a trip to the vet. We went with the preconceived notion it was "stress" from the introduction of the new cat in her life. To our surprise, the vet noticed her thyroid gland was too large; a problem that is common to older cats and Chloie's thyroid was no exception. It needed to be taken care of right way.

We're not wealthy people and the options of today's veterinarian medicine are nothing short of a miracle in the quest to extend the lives of our pets. We wished we could have gone for the removal via radiation but it was just too expensive. We could only afford the medicinal treatments, which were laborious, but still effective in halting the progress of the tumor. It was a period of on-again, off-again employment for me and we hoped that in the future, should my employment come back on-again and if her tumor required removal, we could afford the expensive operation.

The common practice for us now was to check her tumor from time-to-time and that involved examining her under in the lower neck. She would come to show signs of liking her belly fur being stroked and then one day she laid on her back, put all four legs in the air and tilted her head back. After stroking her belly for a while, she would tell you when she had enough by a quick swipe of a paw!

Then it became ridiculous. If she was near you on a couch, chair or a bed, you had to only touch her in the side and she would drop onto her back and demand that her belly be stroked like a dog. This was just insane and unheard of but it demanded a name.

A story from my youth was the answer! I knew a guy who was a bona fide "Hot Rodder" and one of his favorite things he purchased, when in college, was a motorcycle. One day while he was at class, his smarty nephew was visiting his home with his mother. The wind was forecast to be very bad that day, as is common in the east during the month of October and my buddy had to leave the motorcycle at home, because driving in those conditions were too dangerous.

As bad luck would have it, the wind blew the new bike down, regardless of his efforts, to keep it safe. When my buddy got home, he was greeted by the little snot-nosed nephew in an excited and laughing voice, with these words, "Your motorcycle went boom! Your motorcycle went boom!"

"Boom" was the key for Chloie! Like the wind coming along, a poke of the finger and Chloie would fall over. From then on, when we wanted to play with Chloie or just show we wanted to give her undivided attention, we would come up to her and say "Boom Kitty" while poking her with a finger on the side. It did not take long for Pavlov's theory to work with her. After a while, we only had to look at her and say the words, "Boom Kitty" or "Are you a Boom Kitty?" and she was ready for all the affection you could give and roll over on her back. She was now Chloie, "the Cloistered" Boom Kitty.

6

HONEY, YOU'LL NEVER GUESS WHAT I SAW TODAY!

Our horse Marshall lost his battle with his bad leg, the year before. On the very night one of our parents passed away, I would feed little Blackie for the last time. She walked down the driveway as I was about to leave for the hospital. She turned and looked back at me one last time, though I didn't know it would be the last time I would see her. It will always haunt me but I am satisfied she knew what she doing.

So now, with our emotions badly bruised, we had sworn that we would not increase the size of our personal animal stock. No more dogs. No more cats. No more horses. Like the tide that ebbs and flows, so do our best intentions. It wasn't before the end of the spring of 2008 that I saw another cat on our back deck. This cat was different for it had five little kittens following it! She was a mostly gray tabby cat with a white bib, just like Charlotte's. The mother was performing the same ritual I had seen other cats enact on the back of that deck; she was hunting and showing her litter how to do the same.

I counted them twice and the total was still five. They moved back off the deck and down the steps. I quietly moved down stairs and watched them from the back door as they followed the mother with an air of confidence and security. Their little tails were up in the air and they almost bounced along in the patches of taller grass like little deer. I opened the door with just as much caution as before to deter the creation of noises by my actions. My success was rewarded within a few steps out the back door and with camera in hand, I snapped the evidence I needed to make sure my wife would not think I was crazy.

While our emotions were still fragile over our losses of the last few years, we decided to just help them anyway; we could but by no means would become attached to them. This, of course, felt very similar to all the times before. The paper plates were being pulled out again and extra cans of "pate" style cat food were being purchased. We began feeding them on the deck and we suspected they would all run off after a while.

As time would go on, our new plan would take another hit. The dynamics of life were about to come in like a changing tide once again. One of my sisters had been involved with another "Shelter" across the County and she would occasionally hit me up with a test question about wanting another dog or a horse. This time she hit pay dirt.

Our mare, Beary, was a lonely girl without her mate of 20 years and she was acting a little strange toward me and any other being. We had to give her to somebody who had horses to keep her company since horses are herd animals (no matter what you see on TV or in the movies, they do not like to be alone). The other choice was to do what they do in movies and "bite the bullet". That meant getting another horse for Beary. This entire event broke the ice and our new "no acquisition" rule on animals. We threw up our hands and green-lighted the adoption of a horse from my sister's shelter.

Our next move was to catch the little kittens, which had been getting older now and get them fixed. Since Blackie was gone, there was nobody to guard the barn and the feed supplies. One of the lessons we learned by trial and error was that mother cats will ditch their young like all other animals in the wild when they get to a certain age. Our timing was not different at this juncture.

We had not seen a good deal of the mother and she did not call our property her home. She had dumped them here on our property and out of the five, only two had remained; a lighter grey, carbon copy of the mother and a solid grey type with just a little dot of white in the center of the breast at the base of the throat.

The solid grey kitten had always been waiting for me with the food and became quite friendly. He scared off the other cat, we think, and this one grey cat was now the king of the feline world on our property. He would follow you wherever you would go and no matter the task. Just like Blackie in that sense but more so. He would follow you like a dog. Never leaving you out of his sight and if you became stationary, he would find a spot where he could be centrally located to keep watch over you.

Whenever a family member or friend would come over, they would marvel at how much like a faithful friend he was, as he would follow us around the property. He was a real buddy he was. The name was there, "Buddy". I knew it sounded a little cheap and corny but even in a moment of brevity; the choice of "Buddy" spoke volumes to his personality.

A cat never took to a name so fast. It's as if it was his name and we just got lucky in guessing it. He was destined to become an inside cat too. He was so nice we wanted to get him inside, but we toiled with the thought of how poor Chloie would take it. Her thyroid medicine corrected the imbalance in her blood and she was able to defend herself against Charlotte's attacks. She would even start to give as well as she got and a balance had existed in the house for some time. How could we solve this problem? We didn't know it yet but the answer was just a few months off.

7

MISS PRISS DROPS IN TO STAY

Our affection for Buddy, prompted us to build a shelter for him on the deck as winter was approaching. We wanted to make sure he had a place to come to that was safe, since raccoons had decided to move into the area and had engaged in raiding parties on the tack room in the barn.

I fashioned a cat door mounted into the rear window of the tack room, so the cats could come and go in relative safety and assure that the skunks and other ground dwelling wild critters did not have easy access to the sanctuary of the tack room. Raccoons on the other hand, are quite the menace and can be nasty to other animals when it comes to the subject of food. With winter coming on, we didn't want Buddy to be chased out of the barn and have nowhere to go to be warm and safe.

My wife gave me the idea for making a small hutch, which was just large enough to install a small heating pad designed for pets and have safe entry and exit on two sides. This would allow the occupant to make an emergency exit from the hutch, if needed. I added the idea of making a small porch to fit on the entrance, which is facing the sunny side in the wintertime. "Sandwiched" foam insulation between a layer of cedar, tongue and grooved paneling on the inside and exterior grade siding made this unit heavy, strong and water tight. I hinged the roof so that it's easy to access the inside for cleaning. The sun porch is enclosed on two sides leaving one side open for access to the unit. Even without the heating pad, the inside insulation with some towels for bedding keeps an animal quite comfy with their own body heat.

Now, Buddy was all over the property and quite comfortable with the authority that came with it. However, just when things looked to be settled for the winter season, there was a problem. The one cat Buddy had run off had come back but this time she had a little kitten with her. Yet another grey tabby, like her mother and her mother before her, she was learning how to hunt and eat manmade cat food. We also knew the kitten was going to get "dumped" here.

We tried to catch this new mother, but she was very shy and never trusted us the way Buddy had. She was nasty most of the time and quite vocal about it. Buddy tried to run her off; however, she kept coming back.

It was January now and thankfully, it had not been too brutal a winter. The new cat had such an attitude about herself and she would walk away from you with her tail in the air while you brought her food. The whole time, she would add a nasty hiss to her address. Her hiding place was an old ground hog hole in the neighbor's backyard. She would bring the little grey kitten out and eat off the plates of food we left. I would bring them warm water too.

This all worked well for a while, but what if the snow would come? We needed to try to get her close to the house and in the barn or even let her take Buddy's hutch on the deck. We tried everything for weeks to get her to come to the deck. We moved the food just a little further away each time but the kitten would not leave the comfort of the woods. It was too young.

Then we noticed the new cat would come up to the deck when it was feeding time as if to remind us, by clawing the screen door, when we appeared in the kitchen. We decided to feed her up there on the deck. This was a difficult transition and we were always fearful the raccoons would smell the food and show up. It worked and she started to eat on the sun porch but the kitten could not get up on the sun porch. We positioned a cinder block in the right place and up it went onto the porch.

I wish I could say this event had a happy conclusion, but something happened to the kitten. Sparing the details, my lovely wife and I tried to save the kitten at the new local vet, but we were unable. They were so kind to us that they did not charge us for the visit. It was a difficult way to be introduced to a new veterinarian, but there it was.

Again, I witnessed the sorrow of an animal. Animals know loss and experience sorrow. Animals also move on, but they never forget…just like humans. The new cat earned her name from us by her attitude. Although she would be very "stressed" for weeks as she looked for her kitten everywhere, she seemed to keep her "prissy" attitude. A real "Miss Priss" we would call her. We needed to shorten that to something useable, but we never knew how long she would stick around so giving her a long name would have been a waste. It became "Missy" and she would be around for a long time to come as it turned out.

8

A BLUE COLLAR MISSING AN OWNER

A year had gone by and another spring was fast approaching. All things being unequal as they always are in reality, I was paying close attention to the back of the property one morning while enjoying a cup of coffee. I noticed two large cats having a "standoff", right along the edge of the property.

One cat was an orange tabby, which we had seen from time-to-time, but he was quite the wild one. He never tried to make friends with us and always would raid the food bowls if Buddy and Missy were not around. The new cat was one we had not seen before and he stood out as a dark tabby. His back looked a little arched while he walked but it wasn't from being upset or ready to strike. It looked like he had a confirmation problem. In fact, his tail was up in the air a bit. The item that concerned me was that he was wearing a blue collar with a bell on it. He was somebody's cat for sure and his owners let him out to prowl around, which was going to be a problem for my cats, or he had made an escape and took out on his own.

The one thing we try to never think about is that somebody set him loose on purpose. Unfortunately, we have seen this too often.

The orange tabby did not like the situation at hand and after a little contemplation, he sauntered away very slowly as cats will do when in fear they might be attacked. That left the new guy who looked disappointed and sat down   to   ponder   his   surroundings.

We kept a close eye out for him as time was going by. He was not afraid of Buddy, but kept his distance around Missy. Buddy didn't like him much and would always try to find something else to do rather than get to know his new neighbor.

The new cat was very friendly and in no time at all, he found his way to our deck and would look for handouts. This was telling us that he was not being fed by anybody in the neighborhood. We verified this by noticing his hair was becoming a little wiry and dirty. After two weeks, he showed signs of losing weight and along with the weight; he lost that blue collar of his. So now, we knew there was going to be another face to feed.

We had not really been petting him, because we didn't' know his history. My calls to the local shelters and Animal Warden confirmed nobody was looking for this guy through official channels. So, we started to make plans on catching him and taking him in for vaccinations.

His temperament was that of a docile little fur ball when in the company of humans. Before we took him in officially, an old friend of mine from high school was visiting with his daughter Stella. Stella loves animals and the dark tabby loved children apparently. We were walking along the side yard over to the barn to visit with Bay Bear the mare and the dark tabby walked along with us. Before we knew it, Stella had picked the cat up and was squeezing him tight like a doll. You should have seen the expression on the cat's face! He was happier than we had ever seen him. He obviously missed his owners and they must have had children.

I half hoped my friend would take him with them! My old friend grimaced and then gave the order to put the cat down. He looked at me and explained how that would not go over well at home. Well, I understood completely, but at least I saw a side of the cat that told me, he would be a good cat to have around the place, since he was friendly.

Now, I was confronted by the familiar problem. What were we going to call him? We were convinced he was somebody's pet so he must have had a name and we didn't want to confuse him with a lengthy name. We also wanted to keep it in the phonetic tone that cats like. We tangled with the idea of a name but I still had to go back to first impressions or character items in search of a name.

The one item that had set him apart from the rest was when he showed up in the yard. He was wearing the blue collar that he lost after a while. Well, since he really did belong to somebody else first and I wished he could go back to them because he missed being handled so much, I decided to give him a name that always reminded us he was not ours but just visiting. I decided on "B C" as derived from the initials of "Blue Collar" which is now his official name on record.

He's now known as "B C Kitty" and from the very day we started using it with him he liked it. He likes it so much that when you hold him and you quietly say B C Kitty into his ear, he just rubs and rubs his face on your chin.

B C is one of those cats who like to hang on to you

with his front legs wrapped around your neck so you're almost holding him like an infant. Even now when I hold him, I wish he could be reunited with his owners. I know he likes my attention, however, every year when we go to the vet's office for a check-up and vaccines, it never fails that there is one or more children in the waiting room; he will sit up in his cage with big eyes and look to the children as if they might be the ones he knew. I feel very bad for him in those moments. I always wish he could have been, reunited with his family.

He is quite a character, that B C and he has a great heart. I'm glad we took him in even though he doesn't get along with the other cats. You can tell that loneliness and abandonment would have done him in for sure.

9

CRYSTAL, LITTLE BUDDY AND SMUDGY BECOME…

We knew that Missy had her litters in other places and would move them through here most of the time for training and then turn them loose someplace else when she was ready to launch them into the new world. We also knew we missed a few of them. We saw one or two, only briefly, before she took them somewhere else, if some of our other visiting cats were too numerous around the house and the barn.

It was not long before we saw that B C Kitty was never afraid of a little competition. Buddy was the dominant figure around the place. We had not tried to catch him and have him fixed up to this point, because we simply did not have the chance.

Missy had been around in the summer after B C had made us his new keepers. She had three kittens with her when she brought them out of wherever she was hiding them in their early stages of life. She would bring them up to the deck and start teaching them the fine art of eating dry food and how to hunt as her mother had done for her.

By now, I had fixed up more of the barn and remodeled the tack room to something more useable and free of the elements. One of the improvements was to a pane of the back window, which was broken. I managed to cut out a piece of plywood that fit the window frame and then cut a hole in it to mount a cat door. This gave the outdoor cats a way to get further inside a real shelter if they didn't' want to sit up in the barn somewhere. Missy had learned of this place too and it did not take her long before she got those three kittens in the tack room for safekeeping.

It was in the newly finished tack room that I was able to see the new litter up close and personal. We decided to start feeding Missy in the tack room since it would give her and the new kittens more cover from predators and the elements. We also knew it would get them more used to us and probably domesticate them to the extent that we could handle them and keep them vaccinated.

Missy had herself, three beautiful kittens. One was gray, with a little white dot on its breast and looked just like Buddy. The next one had the same gray hair, with four white paws and white hair up the chin over the lower jaw. The third one was a black and white combination that looked almost like the second one except where there was gray hair; this one had black. This one also possessed an unusual area of white that came up over the mouth and up over one side of the nose.

They were all very shy and Missy kept them back under a low-slung wicker chase lounge, we had inside the tack room. Missy herself was still afraid of us and never really ate in our presence until much later. She would wait until I left the food in the bowls and then exited the small tack room.

The small gray kitten, with the Buddy hair, had to have been from Buddy. We were so confident in that fact that we decided to go ahead and pin the label on it. We called it "Little Buddy". Not very original, I admit, but why fix something that wasn't broken?

The other two were giving us the same impressions for names. Their looks were compelling, so, we went ahead and assigned them names on their physical appearance.

The gray and white, was such a pretty looking cat and it had wonderful yellow eyes, which shown like yellow crystals. We decided on something out of the ordinary and strayed from the "e" sounding names and called it "Crystal".

The third kitty had that peculiar white splotch on its face that made it stand out in the crowd. A possible fit might be "Splotch" or "Splotchy" maybe. However, it really wasn't a splotch, you see. It was more like somebody took a paintbrush with white paint and smudged the paint onto the canvas of what would be the kitty's face. So it was here I made up a name for this little gem; it would be "Smudgy".

I was quite comfortable with the choices and for a week or so, my wife was fine with them as well. For some reason however, she had a moment of clarity that I wished I had before planting the names like flags in the ground of my mind. She brought up the question about the gender of the names, in that they may be wrong. Since we had not been close enough to the youngsters to tell what sex they were, it might have been a little premature to assign those names.

So, the big waiting game was on. We thought "Smudgy" was fine and could have been used in either case of male or female, but the Little Buddy and Crystal names, were in jeopardy of being wrong.

We toiled for a bit and then thought of a solution that would work for us and we could gradually change them for their own recognition purposes down the road. In the case of Little Buddy, we would simply use the old Appalachian style of combining names and change it to Buddietta. For Crystal, my wife's thought that adding "Billy" in front of Crystal would make the change easy.

In Crystals' case, it got into trouble around one of the horse's water buckets, when both horse and I approached the barn for a little hoof maintenance. Crystal had been spying on us for a few minutes from behind the big water bucket. Both our draft horse and I knew this and approached slowly but that was too much for little Crystal.

Crystal shot up in the air, about three feet, twice, and landed the first time in the same place he started. His attempt to clear out into to the open for a good run didn't work so he tried it again. This time Crystal jumped almost as high but instead of a trajectory away from the bucket, the little kitty landed squarely into the water bucket.

Luckily, the bucket only had a few inches of water in it. Crystal was scared and its body was stretched up the side of the bucket with its paws trying to get a hold of the lip of the bucket. The frantic pawing did not stop and the little bit of water at the bottom of the bucket was splashing up all over the kitty.

Now, I just want to add what happened next was almost as surprising to me as what was going on with Crystal. Mary, the draft horse, and I, at the same exact moment, looked at each other. I shrugged my shoulders and she blew a little air from her nostrils. Once again proving to me, the animal world is just as capable of reasoning as we are. This was a funny moment and Mary knew it.

I patted Mary on the head and said, "Wait here while I help". In two moves that seemed like one, I let go of Mary's lead rope with my right hand, leaned over, with my left hand, and carefully tipped the bucket over just enough for Crystal to get a good footing. Crystal shot out like a rocket but then stopped. It sat down some twenty feet away, started taking a bath, and looked back at Mary and me as to get an eye full of the big beings that didn't catch and eat the little one. You could tell; it was storing us in its memory as two of the "good ones".

As the weeks went by we noticed Missy had stopped eating with the kittens that were starting to get around on their own. Then one day, Missy went off and there were only the three kittens.

Catching kittens was a new procedure for us and we had it on our calendar that the local animal shelter was holding a rabies vaccination and spay/neuter clinic. We had no real experience with trapping animals, so our learning curve would be a tall one. The use of traps would take some time and we needed to make the clinic. What made it worse was by this time, we discovered the kittens were starting to wander on their own and we might miss the chance to catch them. First Smudgy was missing a few meals and then Little Buddy and Crystal would disappear for a meal or two and only Smudgy was there.

As it turned out, Crystal and Little Buddy were just peas in a pod and they traveled together all the time. You never saw one without the other. Little Buddy was still a real scaredee-cat. After the water bucket incident, Crystal started to come up and rub my legs at feeding time and

Smudgy would too. Little Buddy would stay under the chair and wait for me to leave, but no longer panicked after we caught them and actually did come up and rub my hand a few times.

Therefore, our problem was logistics. Catching them all at the same time was impossible now, so, we were going to have to just trust our luck on the day of the clinic.

Just two days before the clinic, Smudgy stopped showing up all together. We never saw him again, but there were plenty of farms around us for him to call home. It was a shame he never stayed, because it he such a pretty cat.

So, on clinic day, Crystal and Little Buddy were on time for breakfast. I had left two cat carriers in the tack room the night before, with their tops open, so they would be in place without causing a lot of ruckus, which might have scared the cats off.

We tried the old trick of putting the plate of food in the carriers. They didn't like the change in routine and they just looked at us strangely. My wife had locked the cat door from the outside before I went in. We needed to make our move while they were unclear of our intentions.

My wife went for Little Buddy, who by now was sitting on the chase lounge these days. She almost had him too but you never saw a cat scurry and howl like this little one did! I looked down at Crystal and just scooped her up and put her in the box. Crystal was more trusting of me, so not surprisingly; the task was easy. My wife ended up using a large towel and threw it over Little Buddy. A quick scoop with well-gloved hands and Little Buddy was plopped right down in the carrier and ready to go. My wife's experience in handling animals shown through brightly and my suburban sheltered life, once again, stuck out like a sore thumb. However, I must confess, that Fred Astaire had nothing on the moves Little Buddy put down. I never saw a cat run up a wall before that day.

Next stop was to drop them off at the clinic. It wasn't far from our place, but the poor little kittens sounded like it was the end of the world, from their screams and howls.

We dropped them off and waited to hear back from the clinic as to when I could pick them up. After Noon that day, they called and said I could pick them up any time after 3 PM. All was well with my world on that news.

When I got back to the clinic, I was informed that we (I) had incorrectly guessed the sexes of both kittens! Crystal was a he and Little Buddy was a she. This news was sure to have my wife rolling out of her chair laughing, when I called her at work. Well, she did not fall out of her chair anyway. So from that point on, it became "Billy Crystal" and "Buddietta".

Sadly, as that year moved on into summer, we found Buddietta under a tree one morning, badly injured from what had to have been being hit by a car. Billy (as he is now called) was with her when we came out to feed the horses that morning. He came over to us and then walked half way over to where she was hiding. He did that several times and then I followed him to the grim discovery. After a fast trip to that local vet, we brought her body back to the farm. She's now resting right over from Marshall. She really was a beautiful and lively creature.

Billy would go on to be the ruler of the outside roost around here. He's still at it and has to be the nicest, friendliest and most independent cat you will ever meet.

If he's around and hears us walking through our trail in the woods with our dog, he jumps right out and follows along for the entire walk. What a "Silly Billy"! That's what we call him now.

As of this writing, I could swear I've seen Smudgy just a mile up the road at another farm. If it was Smudgy, I saw; he or she looked just fine.

10

BIBBER AND SMOKEY

Bibber and Smokey were two kittens Missy gave birth to, sometime in the late summer, as Billy was just getting his kingdom around the barn set up. Again, she had them somewhere else and this time we think it was at the dairy farm across the street. We would see her bring them across our dangerous rural road in the mornings and hide them in the brush along our front paddock fencing. She would bring them over for feeding, after we put down the food and walked away.

She did things a little differently with these two kittens. That is mostly due to my wife's idea of putting up a doghouse or structure outside, but near the barn for Missy to keep the kittens in. It's now referred to as the "Red Hutch", due to the red painted sides and the red roof awning I put together in front of the structure, to help keep out the elements.

The problem of putting kitties, somewhere safe, cropped up, because Billy had made his home in the tack room. It is typical for spayed and neutered cats to stick close to home, after they have been fixed. Billy made it clear; the tack room was his and would run off just about any cat he did not like. Billy and Missy have this mutual respect for each other and typically coexist with great trepidation, but exist they do.

Bibber and Smokey did end up moving into the tack room with Missy, after they could follow her up to the windowsill and come in that way. Billy would yield the room, after he ate his fill. Once inside, I got a closer look at these two kitties.

Their demeanor was calm, but a little shy. Neither one distinguished themselves behaviorally, so a naming convention was going to have to be limited to appearance features.

Bibber has a great and perfect white bib under his face. It's what you see first before you even meet his eyes. He is a great cat now, who loves our dog more than any other cat we have. The name "Bibber" just sounded right. It had that boy's name sound to it, but it did not have that "eee" ending that cats like, so it was a little experiment for us to see how well it took. We also use the "kitty" suffix sometimes if he is by himself with us.

Smokey was definitely how this cat looked. He was a dark tabby with a little white dot on his breast. His eyes looked lazy and unconcerned about the world around him. If he was in a bar scene in a movie, you would gain the ambience of a smoke filled room. Sounds crazy, I know, but that's the aura he displayed. It did cover the "eee" phonetic convention, so we didn't have to add "kitty" all the time.

Smokey was one we didn't catch for fixing and as we've seen with male cats and those who are not fixed in particular, they go out to make their own territory. We did see him from time-to-time stop in for a quick bite to eat. He would barely allow himself to be in the same room with anybody after a while, as he grew wilder and on his own.

We did manage to catch Bibber and as other litters came along, his shy and inward personality forced him down the street to another barn. We still see him from time to time but we fear for him as he takes an unsafe route to our house.

I've never seen a cat become so happy to see a dog. Bibber is intimidated by other cats, but our current dog "Noel" loves to play with cats. We think the feeling is mutual with Noel about Bibber. Whenever he's around and other cats are near, Noel goes straight to him. She even makes a strange, little, high-pitched, whining, chirp, when sees him. I've never heard a dog make that sound, but Bibber appears to understand it. The face rubbing and the inspecting that goes on is enough to have one concerned the rapture may be close at hand! He always reacts to and puts his tail up when we call him Bibber, so I think the "eee" naming convention, might be expanded a bit, to include an "urrr" sound for cat names.

11

SUNSHINE, SUNNY, SUNFLOWER AND GREENIE

It was spring and Missy had been absent for nearly two months. Smokey had moved on and Billy (a.k.a. Billy Crystal, Silly Billy) and Bibber had become new buddies. They ruled the barn and the yard. It was nice to see them enjoying each other's company. We hoped that since we had our limit on inside cats, that these two, would keep each other company.

Just before May set in, we saw Missy go through her usual movements, when showing up for a meal. We were well versed in her routine and we always had an eye open for her. She would more than likely show herself again with a new litter.

She showed up and did the same thing she had always done and we couldn't figure out why. We knew her habits and she could not have forgotten us so easily. She would not get too close to me before I fed her. She would never rub my legs. She would always give a good warning hiss if I got too close.

Then, it occurred to me after a while, that her new kittens must have been watching me from the edge of the front paddock, where you can find a good collection of short pine trees and ground brush. I looked at the edge of the paddock, but I never could see much in the morning, since she would bring them in from the east. The morning sun would do a fair job of blocking my vision. I trusted her judgment and decided not to try to change her behavior. She knew what she was doing with her kittens and since she had done fairly well with her previous litters, I had faith in her methods.

After a while, she brought the little ones out. She would take them to the same jumping coop first, as a halfway point. Then she shuttled them the rest of the way, to one of the two kitty condominiums I had built, by expanding pre-made doghouses with roofs and polycarbonate glass windscreens.

I needed a way to feed them in foul weather, so their food would not be spoiled and allow them to eat in safety. I made sure they were high enough, so I could easily bend down and place the food while making a quick retreat if need be. It also allowed me to leave food there if they were too shy or if I could not be around for some reason to feed them on their regular schedule.

By this time, the only modification we could see in Missy's behavior was that she trusted us a bit more than each time before. She brought up four little ones to the nearest hutch. We could see a lot of brown and white in this litter except for one, which looked exactly like Smokey. It was quite a batch of little puffballs, with tails waddling across the paddock and with Missy walking close alongside.

This time, they beat me to the little hutch, before I could lay out food. It was also nice to know how many mouths I was going to feed. There was a small pile of fence boards right behind the hutch and next to the paddock fence. All except for Missy, took a quick skedaddle up under the pile, as I walked slowly from the house over to the hutch.

Missy acted a little animated when I drew close. She started rubbing the post to the hutch roof, turning back and forth with her tail in the air. You could see she was showing the little scared faces belonging to the kiddies, hiding under the pile of lumber, that all was well and my presence was a good thing.

I made sure not to make any sudden moves and I didn't look for the kittens. I knew they were watching every twitch and move I made at this point. I just kept my attention focused on Missy and started to slowly pour out some dry food into one of the bowls. Then, I gently popped the canned pate' cat food open and laid that out in two separate dishes. I knew Missy was going to try to show them how to eat prepared food, as she had done with all of the others.

By now, I was a little overwhelmed with the cat naming duties. I asked my wife to step in and do the honors. She gladly accepted and took a while to let their personalities and features gel into her mind. She took a few days and started feeding them. Missy was quite familiar with my wife and displayed the same assurance to the kittens as she had done with me.

My wife liked the whiskers on this batch of kittens. They were long, prominent and full around their entire face. They appeared to have equal length as well. My wife loves animals and enjoys taking care of them. She gathers up warmth every time she gets to make one of the little ones happy, by providing food and a little shelter. It is as if she gets a "blue sky and sunshine" mood when she's tending to the animals. It was no surprise to me, when she started putting names forward for my consumption and comment that were inspired by the sun in the sky. Since we had three girls and one boy, the selection of weather and element related names was easier, I suppose, than if we had the reciprocal of that ratio.

The boy's name was "Sunny". He was a tabby and colored almost exactly like our B C kitty. He had a most spectacular set of white whiskers and eyes that were warm.

Two of the girls, were easy enough, as they were multi-colored. They stayed with each other all the time, one had very earth tone colors, and the other had a more calico type of color scheme.

"Sunshine" would be the name given to earth toned kitty. She also was the most vocal of the group. The combination of her loud meow and full white whiskers, were like rays of sunshine piercing through the window in the morning, giving you the image of sunshine every time you saw her.

"Sunflower" is the name we gave the calico styled kitty. Almost like a sunflower, with her face having big petals made of whiskers and multi-colors in her face that made it more round looking.

The last girl was a little more trouble for my wife to keep in the same naming convention. Of course, I wanted to get them named as soon as possible. I like to address them by their names, as often as I see them, to get a rapport going.

This little girl had one great distinction from her siblings and as far as I could see, any other cat I had ever seen before. She had the greenest eyes. You could almost see her soul inside of them. It was a quick thought on my part, but as I have learned in life, your first hunch is usually your best.

After making the proposal to my wife, she noted the lack of solidarity with her naming convention, but agreed with me that her eyes were of great note. We agreed that it would do for the time being or until we could come up with another name, that would match the rest of the litter.

So far, she's still called "Greenie". In fact, whenever we see her, we call her Greenie or Green Greenie or Greenie Green Greens. It is silly notion I know, but boy does it get her talking! She starts following you, puts her tail in the air and begins to tell you all about what's on her mind. I am sure it's usually about food, whether or not I'm arriving late with her meal.

As time wore on and they grew and started to interact with our other cats and the cats in the neighboring area, we would see less of them. At this point, I will not go into too many details, but once again, I made a grim discovery.

I was feeding the new group and noticed one of them missing. Greenie and Sunny had paired off together some weeks before, as did Sunshine and Sunflower. On this morning, Greenie was at the blue hutch alone and Sunshine and Sunflower were at their usual places at the red hutch. I knew Sunny's absence was trouble. I could feel it in my bones and I think Greenie knew it too. She wasn't hungry and just kept pacing around a bit and whining.

I found Sunny some 200 yards away down our rural road. He was only a foot away from the guardrail. I don't want to say somebody aimed for him with their vehicle, but it was hard not to think it. He now rests down in our lower field near that crossing.

Sunflower and Sunshine would leave together more often after that but Greenie was alone now. She became very anti-social and rather mean to everybody except my wife and me. Greenie is the only one who still shows up more often than not. Sometimes, she'll stay for weeks at a time and disappear for just as long.

Sunflower suffered from an abscess in a front paw the following winter and returned home after being away for almost six months. We made her feeding arrangements in one of our equestrian jumping coops. She was a little more cautious of us but after a few days of repeating her name at feeding time, she was the same old Sunflower. We fixed her up with antibiotics. After she was back to normal, a few weeks later, she took off again and we've never seen her since.

As I am writing this chapter, I am happy to report that Sunshine returned almost five weeks ago. She doesn't mingle with Greenie and eats separately, but in the same section of the stable with her. She still knows her name and started talking to me the very first day, once she recognized my voice and the way I pronounced, Sunshine Kitty! She has grown up to be quite a pretty kitty in deed.

12

Buffy, Tippy, Trooper, Scooter

It was two fall seasons ago, that we noticed Missy, acting as though she was nursing again. We didn't see where she had the new litter, but like always, we knew they were around. Their location would soon be revealed as winter was coming. Missy appeared uninterested in bearing the burden of waiting for them to get old enough to teach them the ritual of our daily offerings. She wanted to get them off on their own soon, so she could be settled for the winter.

Right about this time, Sunshine, Sunflower and Greenie, were still getting settled down around the barn. They really weren't interested in their mother bringing another group of kittens around to compete for food. We were "maxed out" for eating spaces. Missy was still the dominant one of the crowd and as she brought up her four new kittens to eat, she started to butt out her other litter. This started a separation of the cats from their home that would have lasting effects.

However, the task was to get the new kittens fed and then eventually caught. This time, I swore, I would catch Missy. This business of making kittens had ended and I was going to have to outsmart this little cat to accomplish that goal.

At the same time, in the back of our minds, we were thinking of names for the new kittens. So we started looking at their characteristics. They all had grey base toned colors. Three were tabbies and one was yet another spitting image of Buddy as was the late Buddietta. It was a solid grey, with the little white splotch on the breast under the chin.

They were all still small, but stable in their walking, so perhaps, that's why Missy felt they were ready to let go, sooner than the other litters we had seen. Because they were so steady and surefooted, I thought, it was fair enough for us to think about their names as well. I could trust their movements to be the same ones they would make as they got older and if we chose their names on physical behavior, they would not betray out choices. Our instincts were good here.

I didn't want to try guessing the sexes of the kittens, since I couldn't get that close to them. We were going to have to trap them first and have them fixed. However, this time, I knew, I was going to catch Missy.

In the past we were using traps lent to us by our local SPCA and their local "Catch and release" teams. I tried to get Missy in one of those traps. They're quite simple in design, but she was too smart for us. She wasn't about to go crawling down some long cage to get her food. She was quite happy with catching her meals, if she had to, and she valued freedom greatly.

At this point, I had to give Missy credit for reasoning and memory. She saw those traps and started away from them quickly. So, my theory on this was, she knew what the other traps looked like and knew how they worked, but she might not recognize a trap of a different style. It was worth the gamble to buy one of the more popular, commercially available traps and chance it. She had to stop having kittens at any cost.

I lined up the SPCA traps together, four abreast, for a couple of days, with the doors propped open. I put the food for the kittens in one end of the cages and after a few days, they became accustomed to going into the cages and eating without fear of anything happening to them. We also put towels over the top of the cages, which gave the kittens a sense of security.

The traps for the kittens were sitting next to the blue hutch and I set up the commercial trap, some thirty feet away, next to the red hutch. That had a towel over it as well. Missy was suspicious of it at first, but then gently, worked her way into the trap to eat.

After several days, and having called ahead to make sure there would be a vet available at the clinic for spay and neuter work, I was ready to set the traps. Like clockwork, they all went in to their cages and five hours later, with the help and generosity of the Fauquier SPCA, they were ready to bring home and watched for twenty-four hours, before we turned them loose.

All went well after twenty-four hours and we let them out into the front barnyard. They were all very hungry and I had food waiting for them in their usual eating spots. They ate as if nothing had happened to them. From here, we could now decide which names were going to be assigned to Missy's final litter. This was also easier since, we learned their sexes from the SPCA. We had three boys and a girl.

Going on our observations, we formed a few

opinions as to possible names, but their color configuration was a bit of a challenge. Then, my wife was filing the SPCA papers and noticed the color description of the girl, as it was noted by the office personnel. The color was listed as "buff". Now, we looked at a photo I was able to snap of her, just a few days before and in fact, she did have this wonderful "buff" background color to her grey tabby stripes. My wife aptly applied the name "Buffy". I liked it and had no objections so it was settled.

It just so happened, that Buffy was what I read about in the cat adoption community, as a "type A" kitty. That is, she was the first cat of the bunch to approach me and rub my legs and shoes at feeding time. She also let me pet her almost immediately afterward.

It was in this period, that Missy was still trying to figure out what happened to her. We could see her personality change almost immediately and I was a little concerned that she would not get to complete her training with the new cats. That fear was alleviated quickly, as Buffy took charge of the group of four cats.

She started to push the others towards me at feeding time, out in the open under the canopy, as I would lay out their food in the bowls and dishes. It was here that, I formed my opinion on the names of the other three.

It could have been easy to name them after a comedy group or for the namesake of a certain popular, national automotive repair and parts chain, but I knew, I could do better than that. Since two of them looked like identical twins, with small exceptions, that, you get to notice over time and one of them looked just like two other cats we already had, I decided to use the convention of behavior, to create their names. I also decided to give them their names on a first-come, first-name basis. Whichever cat decided to be friendly enough to me and rub my legs, would get his name next.

The next cat to be named, was one of the twins, but he had more of that buff color in his background like that of his sister. He warmed up to me quickly and at one point, he and Buffy were competing for my attention. It can get difficult to walk some times when you have cute, little cats; rubbing all over your feet and legs, but it's a lot of fun just the same. This second cat had a little trick, that, I had not seen in other cats before. Every time he would approach me and rub my legs or shoes, he would give the appearance that he wanted you to reach down and pet him. The only trick was, as you would lean over to pet him, he would flop onto the ground like a sack of potatoes and tip over on his back. There it was, "Tippy".

Tippy was so used to his name that if he heard it and he was in front of you, he would just tip over on his back and look up at you. He is another one of those sweet cats that doesn't like to compete. When I see him around the property, I call out to him, "Tip, Tip, Tippy!" He just rolls over where he stands, even to this day.

The next cat was a funny one. He wasn't as sure about himself around me as Buffy and Tippy, but he loved to hide in the boxwood bushes and jump out at our legs as we walked by. Then, he would run around and scoot back into the bushes. He even loved to launch his fake attacks on the other cats and that included Billy and Bibber, whenever they happened to be around.

That kind of "scooting" around, looked to be a good source for a name, so the grey kitty received the name "Scooter". I also use variants of his name, such as, "Scooty" and "Scooty Scoot". He likes them all now and he's another great cat that just loves all the attention he can get.

This left only one more and he was a shy little

dickens. He would follow his siblings around all over the place, like some kind of shadow. He would parallel them, but staying behind the cover of objects such as trees, bushes, even parked cars, and fence posts. He would hide under the blue hutch until I walked away from feeding.

Buffy tried very hard to get him to come out and eat with her. In fact, they had paired off like Greenie and Sunny. Buffy was much stronger in their security and surroundings than the other and she took on the job of looking after him.

He was never late for feeding however. I always felt he wanted to trust me and he kept trying to, all the while, moving around with military like strengths of training. He was a real trooper, if I ever saw one. And so, his name became "Trooper". It still is and I use no other names, as he's still just as jumpy as they come.

Sadly, and I hate to say it, since the words of that one volunteer ring in mind, about not being able to save them all, tragedy happened again for us one fall afternoon. My Buffy was injured badly and by the early hours of the next morning at an emergency animal hospital, we lost our poor Buffy.

I will tell you that, since her brothers saw her in her injured state, before I got to her, after she had made it back to the blue hutch, after the injury had occurred, they knew something was wrong and they knew she was gone after we came home without her. They knew they had lost her, forever.

They also somehow, saw where I buried her, near where I buried our horse Marshall and little Buddietta. For several days, they laid on the little mound of dirt over her grave. They would do it right after they ate their meals. They would always play together after eating. Yes, my friend, they are smarter than you think and don't ever believe any different.

I was worried mostly about Trooper, but he clings to his brothers for guidance now. They generally keep him in line, but he, out of all of them, sticks very close to home base. To this day, all three are around the house a lot and they have moved up to the recently expanded deck   quarters.

13
NOEL

In this last chapter, I wanted to dedicate a little time to our recently adopted dog. It was two years ago, as of this writing, that we had been thinking, we were ready for another dog, since it was obvious my career in the computer field was gone forever and writing would be a mainstay of my future. Whether I would be successful at writing, was not really the concern, but that, I would be home a lot and having a dog around would help break up the day and make sure I would get out of the house, every now and again.

My sister, Patricia, volunteers at the Middleburg Humane Foundation, which is a fantastic shelter for animals of all kinds. She had often checked with us, to see if we ever needed to pick up a dog, since they always had plenty to adopt. Until now, we had not been ready, since the death of Zorba was so traumatic for us.

One day we were in the neighborhood of one of the big chain pet stores and wouldn't you know it, they were having an adopt-a-pet showing of animals from my sister's shelter. By chance, I had visited the Foundation's website a few days before. What a coincidence! I also had, by coincidence, sent my sister an email on an unrelated subject, but thought I might ask her to inquire of this one particular dog, we saw on their website. It turned out; they were going to show that dog with a lot of others at the pet store that coming Saturday. We thought it couldn't hurt, so, we stopped over, on our way through to another store.

We saw Noel (pronounced Noëlle), and she was very listless and not interested in anybody. The other dogs there were happy, excited and couldn't wait to be petted and get all the free time out of the dog pens they could. It was quite apparent, that whatever happened to Noel wasn't something bad enough that she thought she deserved to end up being cast into a shelter, with other dogs. She didn't want to be with anybody there. If a dog could look depressed, it was this one.

My wife and I were not sure about her. We inquired more about why she had been given up to the Foundation. It turned out, Noel was born at the shelter and was adopted as a puppy, but the family who owned her, had another dog and small children and had just been involved in a move. There were other circumstances as well, but we could tell it was probably psychological trauma and just maybe we could give her a try. We thought a few weeks of life on the farm and open running and chasing the ball, along with our penchant for spoiling our pets that she would come around. The biggest question was how well she would do with our cats.

To the Foundation's credit, they had a complete profile on Noel and one of the items they listed was, how well a prospective adoptee does with other animals. The family she came from, had cats and she supposedly had been fine with them, but the Foundation gave us a demonstration with one of their resident cats, just to make sure.

Noel was her name when we adopted her and we saw no reason to change it. She answers to it. It may be the only thing that links her to her past. She might think of it as her beginning, in this world. Call me crazy, but she's been a fantastic dog and she has us trained extremely well. She absolutely loves her cat friends and I think they love her too.

I wish that all the children and pets that need adoption, will find their way to a warm and loving home. Please, do what you can for their cause. Find a child or pet adoption organization near you and give of yourself as best you can in any way you can. They all need our help. A little help will go a long way.

Now if you will please excuse me, it is time for Noel to give me my afternoon walk!

14

A Closing Thought

During our ordeal with Buffy at the Emergency Veterinarian Hospital, we witnessed a miracle and disaster in the same event. This event is tightly packed, with a lesson, for anybody who gets their pets ID Chipped.

Two sisters came in to the admitting room with a medium sized dog. The dog was healthy and happy and rather excited, but very nice in demeanor. The sisters found the dog in their yard and noticed it had a chip under its skin. The animal warden told them to go to a veterinarian to get the chip read, so, they had shown up with the full expectation, that they would instantly get their answer.

The hospital was more than happy to read the chip, but to everybody's surprise, the chip only had the ID number and the contact number of the company, which holds the information on the pet.

It took a while for the personnel to find the company and at that hour of the day (11:00 PM), they could only leave a message. An hour later, the company called back with an address for the pet that was 1,500 miles away from where we were. The thinking at that point, was that they might try during the next day, to find the veterinarian who inserted the chip, in hopes they would have a forwarding address.

The hospital then told the girls they could take the dog home and wait to hear from them. The girls asked how long they would have to wait to see if the owners could be contacted, before the dog would be up for adoption. The hospital suggested, that if they wanted to take the dog, and a reasonable amount of time had passed and no word of the owner had turned up, then they thought it would be fine for them to just keep the dog.

We never found out how that event concluded, but I would bet, those sisters ended up with the dog, since the last known address was so far away. Our imagination was full of ideas as to how this little dog came to such a fate. One lesson was obvious, if you go to the trouble of having an ID Chip inserted into your pet, make sure that if you move, you need to contact the company that holds the information and get it updated to your new address and phone number. If you don't, you might lose your pet to somebody else. If it happens to be us, then you can be sure, it will get a good name.

PHOTO GALLERY

Chloie

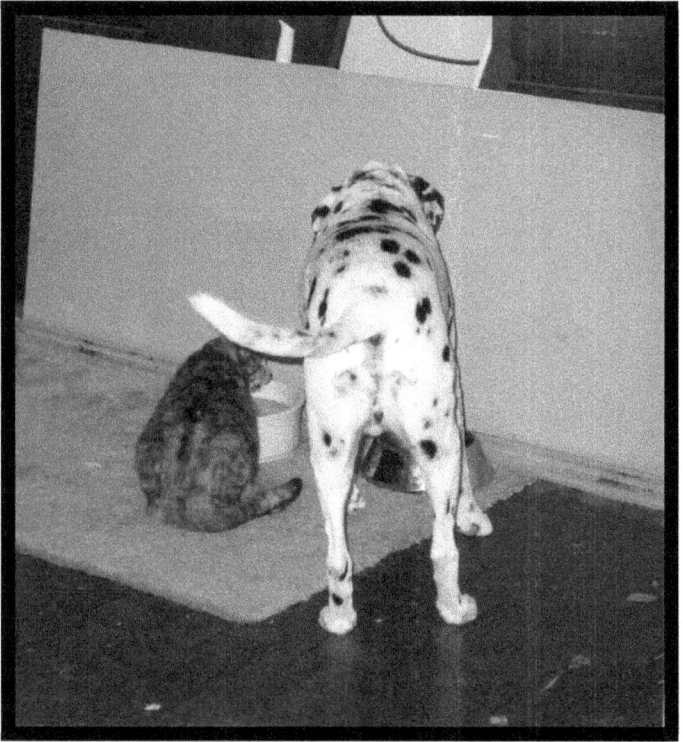

Zorba and Chloie at the water cooler

Zorba and Chloie on a cold winter day

Chloie and Zorba together for ever

Blackie

Buddietta watching over Billy

Chloie meets Buddy for the first time

Billy looking for his dinner

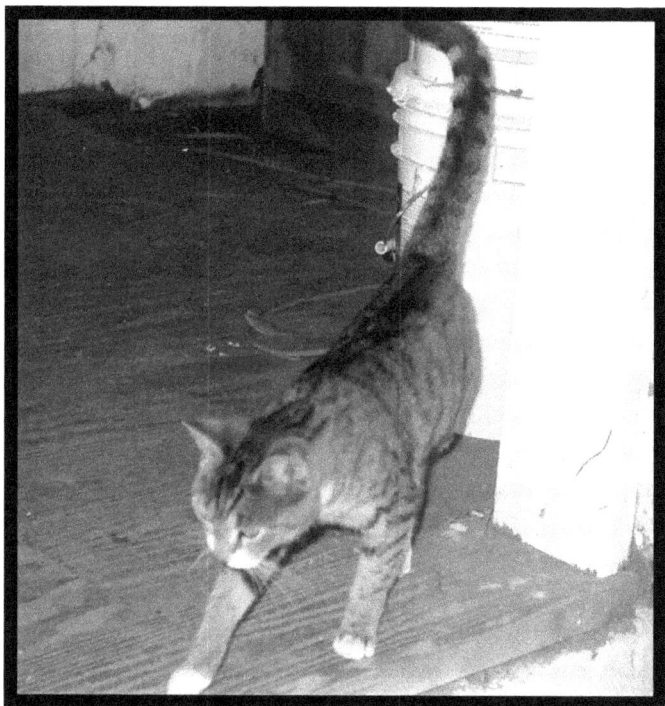

Charlotte before she got her name

Buddy is safe in his basket

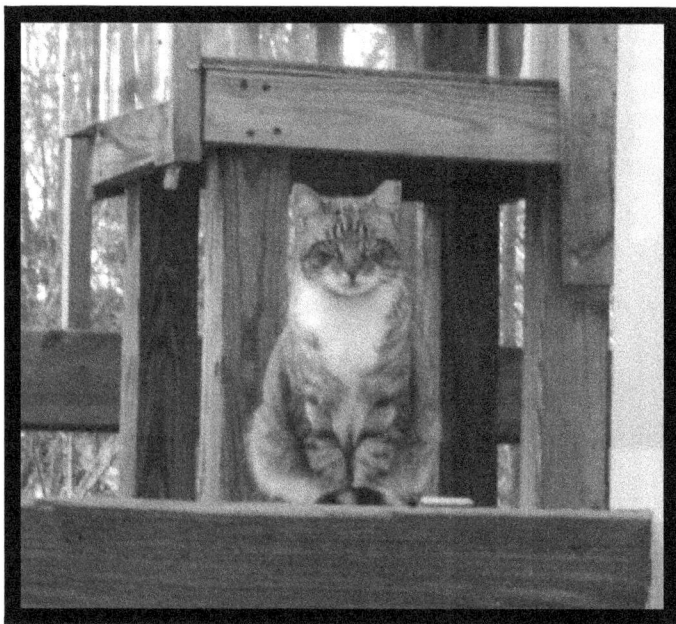

Bibber is waiting for his dinner

Buddy relaxing

Greenie

Sunshine looking cloudy

BC supervising my work

Buffy

Buffy herding Trooper

Trooper keeping tabs on Tippy

Tippy keeps our truck purring

Noel's first night in her new home

Scooter greets Noel
(Scooter is always a blur for the camera)

ABOUT THE AUTHOR

V. R. Agnelli, started writing after a long career in the private sector which came to an end in the 2008 recession. He has many books on the drawing board but while he has been busy preparing to write these future books, he wanted to pay tribute to the work his wonderful wife has accomplished by opening her heart and their home to the animals who could use a little help.